Praise for *Fermentations*

I0795325

"Salvatore Marici's keenly insightful poems sink into our subconscious, ferment and transform themselves into more profound perceptions of the universe. Whether set in a grain mill, or little Sicily in Chicago, or on the banks of the Mississippi River, Marici grounds us in the local—the soil, the fruits and vegetables, the grains and meats of the natural world. At the same time, *Fermentations* masterfully gives us a taste of what lies beyond the horizon."
—Mary Swander, Poet Laureate of Iowa

"In *Fermentations*, Salvatore Marici displays a wide range of empathy, inhabiting not only human speakers, but animals and single-celled organisms, among other creatures. And it is his empathy that guides his most successful poems—consider, for example, "Amoeba's Ego," which ends with: "My greatness / wants more of me. / So, I cut / myself in half." Not only are those lines funny, but they speak to the pain of being overwhelmed by egocentrism. At a time when we're are told every day that the only being that matters is the self, these poems are potent and valuable."
—Shane McCrae, author, *The Animal Too Big to Kill*

"Sal Marici's *Fermentations* rings with the spirit of the great poet, Stanley Kunitz. He fills everyday details with terrific music and insight. These are bright, dymanic poems."
—Terrance Hayes, author, How To Be Drawn

"The 'Fermintations' of Salvatore Marici's poems are the nearly impossible and necessary release of heat, some generosity of insight and meaning amid the confounding circumstances of our lives today. The erotic, the fantastic, the mundane, and the banal all live in these poems. Marici's applies ordinary daily language to the extraordinary, where with a little time, a little good soil, the reader can enjoy the ripened fruit of his remarkable vision. These are poems worth coming back to, again
and again."
—James Brock, author, *nearly Florida*

"2017 looks like a good year in Marici Gardens. Using his yeasty imagination, Salvatore Marici has turned a bountiful crop of ideas, events, places, and people into a lush book of poems. D.H. Lawrence once wrote a friend, 'Whatever the unborn and the dead may know, they cannot know the beauty, the marvel of being alive in the flesh. The dead may look after the afterwards. But the magnificent here and now of life in the flesh is ours, and ours alone, and ours only for a time. We ought to dance with rapture that we should be alive and in the flesh.' Nearly all of Sal Marici's poems in this volume celebrate, 'alive in the flesh' And he makes the writing of those poems sound like such great fun that you may want to start a garden and do a bit of fermenting yourself."
—Roald Tweet, Professor Emeritus of English, Augustana College

"Observation through a poetic lens is the essence of *Fermentations*. It intoxicates the ordinary and we escape into Sal Marici's mindset of what is and what is not."
—Marc Kelly Smith, founder of the International Poetry Slam movement.

"The poetry collected in Salvatore Marici's *Fermentations*, holds tight to a narrative which like a voluptuous garden, requires constant attention to detail and language. Each poem that Marici plants, grows, and harvests in Fermentations is anchored in rich syntactical soil and sunlight. Fermentations, is full of lyrical meditations on migration, pop-culture, religious wonderings, hunger and war of the body, soul and land. The reader is left well fed and satisfied. Poem after poem, Marici serves up language full of energy and delivers a poetics that is as aesthetically pleasing as a fine meal from a five-star restaurant. Get ready dear reader, the table has been set—enjoy the meal."
—Xavier Cavazos, Poetry Society of America National Chapbook Fellow

"*Fermentations*, by Salvatore Marici, celebrates earthiness in all its forms, mostly the gustatory. These unpretentious, potent poems remind us to resist the plastic temptations of the consumer economy that has all but overwhelmed us. This collection, enjoyable to read and ripe with meaning, amounts to an argument for the slow path forward."
—Kelly Daniels, author, Cloudbreak, California

"When popped open, Sal Marici's poems, like variously filled, various sized jars on the shelves of a fruit cellar, emit sour or sweet scents promising crisp or chewy bites. Well-seasoned, his poems pack satisfying aural punches, often doing without articles and punctuation. They bring the reader into an unexpected and unsentimental appreciation of the mundane through energetic use of alliteration, assonance and consonance; Marici coaxes, raises, and subdues sounds like a veteran conductor. Sample two bites from a jar labeled "Concourse K Food Court": "The other lunchers crunch fries, bite burgers./Their tongues lick salt sugar on lips." You won't leave his book hungry."
—Nancy Hayes, English Department Chair, Saint Ambrose University

"Salvatore Marici again sinks his mind's fingers deeply into the stuff of life, touching a diverse and random sampling for his latest, irresistible gem, *Fermentations*. From edibles ("Baked Collage") to aesthetics ("As the Late Afternoon Settles"), Marici beguiles us to follow his complex trail of sublime universal experiences through his special interpretive vision. Bubbling with whimsy, seriousness, wistfulness, darkness, the ever-shifting content mirror the fluidity and constant change of a grand, creative fermentation. And, as fermenting transforms sugars to alcohol, Marici's organic, minimalistic layerings of words transform the readers' perceptions to heady results. Sometimes with a 'tween the eyes directness, at other times, elusive as a peripheral flicker, *Fermentations* will entice each reader to revisit its bounty of poems many times. Such visits will bear such sweet differences as the same vineyard's harvest produces different vintages from one season to the next. Salute!"
—John Busbee, President/Host/Producer for The Culture Buzz

"In his new collection *Fermentations*, Salvatore Marici brings his agronomist's sensibilities to locations as varied as Belize and Guatemala, to the upper Mississippi River Valley and Chicago's North Side. In every location, his sensual perceptions highlight our relationship to the natural world surrounding us. Reading these poems is like meandering through a garden of luscious plants and food. Marici has a constant eye on our cultural relationship with what can be grown, and the planet we live on and care for."
—Felicia Schneiderhan, author, *Newlyweds Afloat*

"Salvatore Marici serves up a banquet of rich sights and smells and flavors in his new collection *Fermentations*. He embraces a wide world, from Paris, Chicago, the Middle East, Chinese prisons where men sleep forty to a cell, the Beatles, Carl Sandburg, Venetian boys. Even his own personal memories feel timeless: 'tenants pay rent to Grandpa with dried fruits.' Read this collection and know the pleasures of preserving summer's bounty for spare winter months: 'I will inhale the perfume tonight.'"

—Stephen Frech, author, *The Dark Villages of Childhood*

Fermentations

Salvatore Marici

Ice Cube Press, LLC
North Liberty, Iowa, USA

Fermentations: Poems of garlic, bread, erotica, nature, mundane

Copyright © 2017 Salvatore Marici

Isbn 9781888160253

Library of Congress Control Number: 2016XXXX

Ice Cube Press, LLC (Est. 1993)
205 N. Front Street North Liberty, Iowa 52317
319-594-6022 www.icecubepress.com
steve@icecubepress.com twitter: @icecubepress

No portion of this book may be reproduced in any way without permission, except for brief quotations for review, or educational work, in which case the publisher shall be provided copies. The views expressed in *Fermentations* are solely those of the author not the Ice Cube Press, LLC.

The paper used in this publication meets the minimum requirements of the American National Standard for Information Sciences—Permanence of Paper for Printed Library Materials, ANSI Z39.48-1992.

Made with recycled paper.

The following poems appeared in the exact or similar version in these great magazines, anthologies, and broadside:
"Seeker for the Masses"—Broadside Alliance for the Arts made a Broadside with this poem; "The Merge: Chicago Near North Side 1920s and 30s"—*Prairie Gold;* "Your Choice"—*Circle Magazine*; "The Height and Fall of Little Sicily"—*Prairie Gold*; "My Cousin Anthony"—*Penny Ante Feud*; "Continuous River Towns"—*The Visible Cities Blog*; "Captured Harvest"—*Spillway*; "Stuck after six hours of Socializing"—*Penny Ante Feud*; "Tantric Dance in the Drum Circle"—*Nefarious Ballerina*; "Contortion"—*Oysters and Chocolate*; "Suppose"—*Aberration Labyrinth*; "The Crave to Purge and Keep"—*Community poetry 2015 blog spot*; "Buon Appetito" and "Drive Thru" are forthcoming in the Main Street Rag Publishing's anthology with the theme of fast food; "Blemish Cleansing"— *Earth's Daughter* with the title "Treasuring Home Grown Garlic."— *Toasted Cheese Literary Journal*, "Amid Life and Spilled Wishes"—*Voices of BHC,* "Morning Rituals and Concourse K Food Court"

Thanks to:
John McBride, Steve Semken, Guru Jah, Deajh Ray, Midwest Writing Center, Mari Messer, George Longenecker, and Kathy Negaard.
All who helped me directly with this book or kept encouraging me to write and keep my voice.
And to Ice Cube Press and other Indie presses.

In memory to:
Thomas Lux, Bruce Carter, George Mathon, Danna Cobb Paglino, and Henry Klingman.

"It is impossible to have a healthy and sound society without a proper respect for the soil."

—Peter Maurin

Table of Contents

Invitation to Enter

> The Gate of Hell, *influenced by Dante's* Inferno, *is a Rodin's sculpture that stands at 6m high, 4m wide and 1m deep. It contains 180 figures.*

Handmade nails
with rusted heads
nailed her bronze face
on an oak door.
Tangled grape vines
dangle from her head.
She speaks four hundred years of
Olive, lemon groves
grow on hillsides.
Wine pours from barrels
in people's homes.
Women bathe under Sicily's sun.
These tales she has seen, done,
lure my hand
to lift the ring beneath her chin,
worn to fit my palm by grabs of others.

But when the sea brings storms
I hear from her lips
cries of tormented souls
like those Rodin carved
on *The Gate of Hell.*
Their tears scald my hand.
Handle crashes
against strike plate.

Morning Rituals

4:15AM my hand slaps the black radio
hushes deafening decibels of chamber music.
Seven hours of dreams go.

Wrapped in red fleece throw
I a Buddhist monk meditate
to rattling registers, southern winds shake
thirty minutes later I turn over bedspread,
two blankets, sheet. Mediterranean climate
settles around my nudity.

Dressed like a BC Greek Olympian
on a rowing machine, I compete
as David Bowie sings.
Silent channel 6 spectators cheer
via satellite for forty minutes.

Sicilian stove espresso pot
spits four shots of crude oil
through a pipe into its top chamber.
Caffeine, adrenalin, generic Prozac
vest me. I a Roman Senator
commands with a flick of my wrist.
Hot water steams my bathhouse.
My slave Cascade scrubs my back.

I a knight suiting up in armor
white shirt with blue strips, black khakis,
and blue tie
for the tournament with the Commander
of the Joint Munitions Command
packed with power point presentation.

6:30AM Moe, Curly, and Ruby Tuesday
sit by the kitchen door
tails like windshield wipers wipe
oak finished laminated floor
tell me to stay at home
fantasize in my poetry.

Car keys in my hand
I frown.

Apollo Comes - Morpheus Leaves

when sun's rays
pry cracks
where dreams leak.

From the Ether

I. Scent before Rain

Lightening zaps.
Ozone downdrafts.
Clean sheets cast freshness
to nostrils.

II. Scent after Rain

Aromatic plants;
lavender, cedar, violet, mint
exude oils. Blood of gods
drips on dry rocks, soil
where droplets lay
until raindrops kick
into air, an aerosol spray
of blended perfume
like bursting Champagne bubbles.

III. She Channels Luminosity

Silk of white sundress
and the air beneath
touch her skin
while barefoot
after a summer shower
in this meadow
returned sun brightens.
Breeze lifts her red hair
weaves into rainbow's orange–band,
brushes an auburn arch.

A star behind her eyes
          sheens them blue.
They match the sky.
She unites palms,
points fingers to cosmos.
Her lips come together and smile.

Suppose

On a sunny Sunday
your foot falls
into woodchuck hole.
The rodent claws skin
between two straps
on your sandal,
drags you. Dust
you slide,
clogs your lungs. Above,

brown-eyed susan and goldenrod
drop seeds. Rain soaks their coats,
swells embryos. Stems burst.
Roots tie knots

so tight
no one finds
the opening.

Stooge in the Guatemalan's Campo

Pheromones shout, "Attack!"
Thirty mouths and 180 legs
scramble over my big toe knuckle
to the blue vein. They nip, inject, sting.
Burning skin swells into a mountain range
as the lava-like invasion spreads.
I scream "ouch-son-of-a-bitch."
My hand smashes and brushes the red dots
while I hop, unzip my knapsack,
untwist the cap of a white bottle
then swallow a Peace Corps-issued Benadryl.

The compesinos laugh
when they see
the gringo pogos
on his good foot
as he holds the bloated one.

Fire ants break jaws
when they bite
natives' tire-thread sandals
and their
inch-thick weathered skin

as they clap
to my jumping beat.

Seeker for Masses

"Poetry is an echo, asking a shadow to dance." – Carl Sandburg

He stabs immigrants with their hunger,
swings their sledgehammers,
tears muscle, rubs bone on bone,
has painted faces walk streets. I hear
accordions, newcomers play. Rhythm moves
my feet as they dance, dances they brought.
I watch people like him and his parents begin
to melt into here.

This man who quit school at thirteen
to put milk jugs on steps chatted
with Kennedy in the oval as the president
rocked his chair. His craft celebrated
with three Pulitzers. Yet today,
writing programs don't echo Sandburg's work
even in dancing shadows of their favorites.

The Merge:
Chicago Near North Side 1920's and 30's

The unified fragrance of tomatoes,
garlic, basil and meatballs
sneaks out opened windows

lingers front porches
of three story brick buildings
where men born in Sicily
sit with young children
on Sunday afternoons.

On the steps,
fathers teach first-borns
English
accented vowels attached
to wave American flags.

Lost Lineage

We put foods
laced, injected
with fake flavors
in microwaves
press buttons
wait for dings.

Then eat at tables
covered with
plastic bags
smart phones
with open apps
where no aromas of
roasting meats,
simmering sauces
rouse taste buds.
Where nobody sits
around tables tell tales.

Concourse K Food Court

Mothers and daughters
wear polyester dresses
of whatever pattern and color
they could get. Aprons' ties
secure their waists

as they cook on wood fires
or propane two-burner stoves
in their houses
or prepare on a grill
made from scrapped metal
before hungry customers.

Corn tortillas layered with
chopped meat from unknown species,
shredded raw cabbage, red sauce dabs,
serve on brown paper
under the sun on bare Guatemala ground
whose dust whirls with a slight stir
where drivers drive old school buses
painted bright red and blue
wait for passengers
10 kilometers east of El Salvador.

While in O'Hare
five Hispanic women
middle age and younger
wear blue scrubs
uniforms of uneducated laborers
only one eats beans and rice
out of a recycled margarine tub.

The other lunchers bite burgers.
Thier tongues lick salt sugar on lips.
They crunch fries boiled
in partially hydrogenated oils
melted like their culture.

Buon Appetito

Teenager voice in the box asks
"Can I have your order?"
The driver replies, "A half pounder
with extra secret sauce
of Thousand Island dressing,
potato sticks dipped
in boiling GMO oils,
three pints of high fructose corn syrup
and artificial flavorings mixed in water.
Also an order of chopped chicken
combined with ingredients
of no natural substances
except salt
pressed into nuggets then deep fried."
He rolls his car to window.
Another trolls like a fish after a lure,
fills his space.

Drive Thru

Patrons wedge fries
between plump thighs
push a quarter
of a half pounder
in stretched mouths. Secret sauce
splatters shirts, blouses, pants.
Twisting steering wheels trigger
soft drink tsunamis.
Forces throw plastic lids.

Your Choice

Mills strip bran and polish grains white.
In minutes, our bodies break bleached cereal
into sugar, enough to fuel semis. Gears grind.
We run red lights and crash into others.
Excitement burns. Hope faith drop.

Whole grain energy
hums, fuels our journeys.
on earth, in cosmos.

Baked Collage

Heat rises the blend
of yeast, flour,
water, sugar.
Mass rises.
Sweetness leaks
until the outside hardens
seals. Crust cracks air.

I chew the craved rush.

The Height and Fall of Little Sicily

A few days before Memorial Day
during 1920s in the Chicago Near North Side
men's shoulders support and their steps sway
a platform where a wood Mother Mary stands.
When back at Saint Philip's church steps
Father Luigi sprinkles holy water.
Parishioners clip dollar bills to the wire aura
purchased permission to kiss the statue.
White robes drape two girls wearing cardboard wings.
Callused hands pull ropes harnessed to their backs.
The angels recite Latin three stories high over
grills scaring black stripes on green peppers' skin,
fennel sausages dripping fat
and the barrels of wine and kegs of beer
the neighborhood's Don provides.
Shops and corners scream, "rat a tat" no one sees.
A cluster of girls in plaid skirts and white blouses walk.
Boys in black trousers, white shirts, and black ties follow.
In one-room grocery stores, twine suspends
pear shape provolone and hard salami from ceilings.
Feet squeak floor planks where wood barrels
filled with black and green olives sit.
Vinegar stains the outside curves. On sidewalks
eggplants and apples display on shelves.
Bakeries sell cannoli and cookie sheets
of white bread splattered with chunks
of tomatoes, mozzarella, and splashes of olive oil.
Puffs of risen yeast and flour harden into crust
steam into the streets.
Men climb boxcars from California,
taste and choose red grapes they press, pour juice
into five-gallon clay containers in kitchens.

Tenants pay rent to Grandpa with dried fruit
the government allocated and Grandma rehydrates,
then bakes. She gives pies to the renters.
The city demolishes those homes
during and after World War II.
Cabrini-Green constructed over foundations
like ruins in Sicily. Saint Philip closes.

AMID LIFE

New immigrants from
North Africa, Eastern Europe live with French
in this working class Paris neighborhood.
During this fall evening
young couples, a few with strollers

stroll the avenue
eat at Little Cambodian,
visit a bistro where people drink
beer, wine and coffee. Two men
raises their glasses, *Tchin Tch....*
Blast drowns the clink. Gust broadcasts
metallic shards. Walls, furniture, flesh
take. Black masked men run
into the ruin carry assault rifles,
shoot anybody with movement.
Outside as if on a carousel
they rotate, clench triggers.
Five bullets pierce a bakery.

Next morning
the Moroccan-born owner
bows his head at a makeshift memorial
across from his store
then turns, walks to the door.
Inside he sweeps slivers of glass,
tapes holes in the store front window.
Then he kneads white dough,
shapes loaves, lets rise, bakes bread.

Sweet goodness sprinkles streets,
the shock breathe.

Messages of Red (Part I)

Bombs rip flesh.
Hearts' squeeze
squirt bright blood.
Ambulances' lights pierce
like stabbing pitchforks.

The Victor at the Gallows

> Saddam killed at least 50,000 Kurds
> possibly as many as 100,000 - U.S. Department of State

Saddam Hussein in cuffs struts
front and behind guards.

Saddam shouts,
Down with the invaders.

A Kurd screams,
"Go to hell."

Hussein hollers,
"Hell, that is Iraq."

Blemish Cleansing

In an opened cardboard box
I flick 200 garlic heads I dug
yank their teeth and chuck them
into the peeler, a pliable tube
my hand crushes and rolls.
I hear cracks
raise one end of the chute.
Skinless cloves fall.

Thin paper and dirt
fingerprints white flesh I pick
and drop in mason jars.
Saltwater fills spaces
where bacteria start to thrive
in wedges
pointed and piled like reefs.

After microbes seized,
small bulbs stain air
with a pungent smell.
Beneath foam
fermenting cloves
stay hard
do not sprout
and know because
they lack girth or
bare brown spots
I did not plant them
to rid their flaws
from future generations

as they sit next to the toaster
watch me scrape one of them
layer after layer on toast to nothing.

Summer Wane in Upper Mississippi Valley

In a sky,
day paints Egyptian blue
an angel fluffs wings
whose breath wafts dry warmth
with specks of coolness.
Pockets of fading-green
spot crowns of trees like bubbles
above cartoon characters
filled with scripts
of leaves' last wishes.
Fallen apples, pears
ooze hard cider, bees slurp.
They brawl in sugared air.
Goldenrod spikes burst
metallic-yellow. Sun scatters lusters
some settle, some suspend.
Pumpkins, butternut squashes,
lie amidst seared vines, split tomatoes.

Then dusk,
a minute before yesterday,
owls' ears trace moles' scurries
who through small eyes
see sunlight dim.

At Dusk

In Davenport Iowa, sleet sinks
into a woman's jacket
stained with street dirt.
She lies on cardboard
shivers heat into concrete.

A man's heavy brown tweed
shields him to his knees.
He sidesteps her
scuttles to a door
his key unlocks.

Inside he flicks a switch.
Lights shine
where moving air
a furnace blows
diffuses warmth
sheds his chill.
He unbuttons his coat.

Christmas Décor Cheer

> *"Nobody got paid anything,"*
> *"If you didn't work, you didn't get food."*
> NPR Morning Edition Report May 29 2014

Mildew-smell fouls
Chinese prison cells
with no window, chair, bed, mat.

Forty men sleep on their sides
like folders stuffed in cabinets.
Each hopes an official picks his file,
brings to a hearing
no one has.

When guards say *the sun shines*
inmates wake stripped to underwear
to stop their clothes soak sweat
when march in place
for an hour. The next ten they squat
push frosted bulbs into sockets
attached to green wires
bosses flog on bare backs
          beat contract deadlines
government has.

My Cousin Anthony

The CEO of a real estate mutual fund
dresses in a black tailored suit
at his nephew's wedding.
As we watch
white people dance
to rap he says,
 I drive
 from my Michigan Avenue condo
 to work instead of walking.
 It saves 9 minutes.
 You cannot buy back time.

This Sunday
the government credits
this millionaire one hour
in the name of saving daylight.
In 60 minutes,
he reads prospectuses, selects stocks
his company will buy and sell
then sips a single malt. He bought
6.7 commutes
with his interest free loan.

Continuous River Towns

Steamboats no longer stop
in towns without stoplights
along the Great River Route
in the upper Mississippi River Valley.
Planners seek investors
who will renovate and erect

strive for quaint ambience
they inject into the passersby
hope they become
spending tourists
or property taxpayers
they convince to stay.

Belize's Ship Builder's Yard in Juxtapose

Ribs of wooden fishing boats
exposed like those of dogs
whose owners feed
two tortillas each day
except no stretched skin, no sparse fur
wrap their bowed wood
while they lay on their backs
as if they want
their hollowed bellies scratched.

Jack Becomes Humble

> The crevalle jack is a voracious predator, it feeds primarily on smaller fishes - The International Game Fish Association

Half of the red lure
hides in Jack's mouth,
rest pokes air.
The tail on his ten-pound body
drums water while he swims
a stationary sidestroke.
His eye stares into sky.

With two hands on the pole
and line over the railing,
Jill prances
to the boardwalk's end
where she left her tackle box
under the tiki's hut.
Jack skims water.

Under thatched roof, Jill yanks pole.
Jack flops on slabs. His gills cough
opened mouth snorts.

Jill's foot holds the line down.
Needle pliers clutch hook
twist un-pierce lip.
She kicks Jack over the edge.

It swims.

Fish Market

While I shop
for freshness
their dead eyes
glaze gray
stare without blinks
goose-bump me
as if I not them
top crushed ice.

State the Last Name

In my condo
I Skype Enrico in Rome.
His Italian-infected English
stretches vowels at the end of words
including those that do not end
with a, e, i, o, u. He says
"Go to the fishermen
buy their fish packed in ice
next to their boats."

Along the coast, I search
for wooden fishing boats dock.
Their catch displayed on stand.
Instead, I see high rises
yachts in marinas,
beach parking.

Half a day
quarter tank burned
I stop in a chain grocery
buy with my credit card
a two pound bag
of King Fish steaks, vacuum sealed,
caught in the wild off China.

I e-mail Enrico, clarify
I live in Naples Florida.

Encyclical

> Temperature's rising
> Can't see no sky
> Can't see no future
> – John Lennon

Shepherds pointed at stars
drew deities. Hubble's photos
spur arguments
                    about our spirituality
          about our beginning.

Here on earth,
Pope Francis speaks.
If we destroy this planet
this marvelous creation
it will destroy us.

Induced Earthquakes – Introduced Poisons

Colonoscopy doctor
shoots gas through tube
in ass bent to intestine.

Recovery nurse tells patient
let it rip. Air rumbles.
Curtains between beds sway,

ground murmurs, shakes
when augers drill soil
then shale
pipes gush chemicals,
sand mixed with water
we could have drunk, used to irrigate.
Force blasts tunnels with cracks.
Fractured bedrock shifts. Fragments fall

in grinders. Sausage stuffers push
ground pork in flushed intestines
stretches casings thin.
E. coli finds pinholes, seeps.
More pressure tears walls. Toxins leak

into springs, drinking wells
from filth thrust in earth.

Altered Development

Tops of garlic stems shoot
green trails. They curve
and sprout white cones
soon to open and become fertile.
My fingers pinch twist snap
them. Flower heads fall
like testicles in scrotums
squeezed through slits
scissors cut
before pubes grow fuzz
on boys in Venice
able to sync lips
to soprano angels.

Garlic Grower's Prize

I walk into the patch, amidst grasses
whose spikes brush my hat's brim
kick straw expose newspaper
first layer of four,
unwanted roots unable to penetrate
invade the seedbed. Hands, dirt creases,
pluck those plants.
My feet, sandals strap
push spade cut
through shield I built.

I unearth a skull
full of white teeth,
first of the 323 I will dig
out of tilth I made from clay
with manure I collected, spread
tilled for nine years.

The head cradles in my palm
as how archaeologists cup a bowl
thousand years old with hairline cracks.
Yet,

as my sweat
adds to humidity
80 degrees capsulate
I wish
the sun would drop
before this mid-July evening does
so I can sit in cooled air.

When people ask, "Give me heads?"
I turn away; mumble, "Screw you asshole."

Captured Harvest

The lifter's jaw dips in pressure cooker
clamps wide rims, lifts jars
places them on wood boards.
We wait to hear lids pop.

This winter when we break seals:
its juices burst a whiff.
We chew swallow summer
our peach tree reaped.

ANOTHER FARM GONE

> Dr. Palmer informs that if you say the word "dirt" in this class, you fail.
> Soils 101- Western IL University

Piles sit next to holes excavators dug.
Soil scientists call these heaps "dirt."
Builders pour in each hollow a cement floor.
Contractors haul dirt, return; sell top soil.

Soil scientists call these heaps "dirt."
Last year corn grew in this ground, soil filled.
Contractors haul dirt, return; sell top soil
new homeowners spread, plant grasses, trees.

Last year corn grew in this ground, soil filled.
Today piles sit next to holes, excavators dug.
Soil scientists call these heaps "dirt."
Builders pour in each hollowed a cement floor.
Contractors haul dirt, return; sell top soil
new homeowners spread, plant grasses, trees.

Reconstruction of a Haven

After a power company
slices the locust treetop
in my front yard for ten years
they saw its trunk.

Rose of Sharon seedlings watch
the shovel's pointed tip cuts lawn,
blade lifts clumps. I pour
black fluffy manure. My fingers
carve spaces
for their four-inch taproots with
root-hair clusters wide as a man's fist.
Palm pats soil, breaks air pockets.
Water can sprinkles. They drink smile.

I see buds sprout, bloom
leaves, pink flowers fall.

In the sixth cycle,
my hand squeezes clipper handles.
Blades snip uncontrolled growth
like how roads and houses sprout
each time a neighbor sells his farm.
My master plan tells branches,
foliage where to yield,
fill spaces. This woven fence

deflects traffic rumbles,
blocks drivers joggers view
of me skyclad as I lie under the sun
with one leg over the hammock.

As the Late Afternoon Sun Settles

> The name Caleb derived from the Hebrew word "kelev,"
> which means "whole hearted."

My arms' swing pace my legs
on a township blacktop.
It takes me
from my house
through fields
of cut stubble and stalk.

A woman walks toward me
with a blond boy who skips
his fifty pounds a few steps
in front of her. Gray streaks
hang from her black knit cap.
Hi, she says then instructs
her grandson to turn back.
He slides his hand in mine.
I hold his right. She holds his left.
She tells me a couple years ago
she saw me read poetry, asks my name.
I tell, ask hers. *Anna* she says.
The boy declares "warm hand."
Again, he says "warm hand."
His name is Caleb.
He does well with eye contact
but he repeats.

We stop at their frame house
where farmers lived.
I wave to Caleb.

Upon his grandmother's prompt,
he lifts his face, looks at me
returns the wave.

My arms hang until
shoes on my driveway
kick gravel.

12:30 PM Thanksgiving Day Ritual

(Dedicated to Helen Biehler)

After I put a turkey in my oven
and before the juices drip,
Kathy and I walk from my garage
across the township's blacktop
to Steve and Helen's farmhouse
built in early 1900's.
My right hand carries an uncorked
Cabernet Sauvignon.

Steve sets four glasses he cut from bottles
on the kitchen table, pours. Helen rolls her walker
to the wooden chair with three pillows. We sit.

She keeps the two prongs
on the oxygen concentrator's plastic tube
stretched from the living room in her nostrils.
Under long and cream polished nails,
Helen's fingers push a white bubble.
A pink pill tears thin tinfoil. Her voice rasps,
I lived with cancer for 10 years.
First time I need to take something for nausea.

Wine slips medicine.
The machine …clicks…sighs.

The doctor wants to try a new chemo
but, we do not know if the insurance
will pay for it.

She lifts and tilts the vessel. Her bottom lip
seals the edge. Red fluid leaves and disappears.
She holds the empty container to Steve.

I don't know if I care.
My body tells me enough.

A couple sips drip
from the upside down bottle.

We got a lot to be thankful for

Residents

Flu killed thirteen year-old girl
generations ago. Her

ghost swings
the seat tied to white oak's limb,

feet drag on ground to halt.
She runs into house,

attaches like a shawl
to a living person, grandfather type

where one year later
while his wife lies on couch

breast cancer kills her
after ten years of tumors

sprout, spread, retract and return.
With a sheet, he shrouds her.
She leaves.

Case for Euthanasia

On my lawn in August
the white oak has no leaves
as if weight of a cold fall rain
felled them.

Beetles carve tunnels
through and under bark.
Pry crusted ridges. Sap glazes
bare wood.

In breezes, arthritic branches grate
moan for gusts to break
their 300-year old trunk.

Windblasts snap rotted wood.

Spectator

After a celebration of life
        for Kathy's friend
        who I knew through her
the mourners meet
in a side room of a Happy Joe's
with pitchers of lite beer
and taco pizza on paper plates.

I sit at a table-laminated brown,
fingers tap its surface,
face two men in their late-sixties
who tell stories from 40 plus years
of drink and golf
cite lines from "Caddy Shack."

Because Kathy asks,
they talk about the present.
Her X says, *I cook for myself*
but not healthy stuff
when my wife works.
I play golf and watch sports.
The other man steadies
his gray synthetic hair. He tells,
I bartend and play golf.

The two men's voices blend.

They chat to themselves
if they should
sit in a bar with a big screen
to watch the football game

or battle the elements
in a stadium
like global leaders
in a nuclear arms summit.

Under table my right foot fidgets.
Jaw clenches a blank face
while I study my finger nails
wish I have a clipper
wait for Kathy to say let's go.

Stuck After Six Hours of Socializing

His Brit accent begins to slip
like suds on the sides
of his empty glass.
He lives in England
but this week he visits
Iowa, his home state,
He talks soccer stats
calls us mates

as I sit on his mother's porch
with four others in Le Claire.
We overlook Cody Street
and the Mississippi
after Tug Fest fireworks
before burnt air disperses.
Cars roll   stop
motorcycles rev   cough
when the light a mile from us
turns green   red.

I shift, face the Englishman
ask a question
to show I have not left
then resume my position
watch for thinned traffic
while their longhair tabby
sits on my lap. I pet.
She sniffs my cat's scent.

Later the tabby curls on a chair.
"*Of course*," she says to herself.
"*Of course, they want to be alone.*
I would too."
The thirteen-pound orange body
wrapped in white stripes stands.
Front legs stretch across the seat.
Paw bats catnip mouse to floor.

Amoeba's Ego

I love myself so much
I will not have sex
with another.
My greatness
wants more of me.
So, I cut
myself in half.

No Peck Scrimmages

In Villa Rica, Paraguay
three hours before sunrise
the moon's luster wakes
dinosaur genes in roosters
whose shined feathers reflect
like silvery scales.

A cock beside a steel door
stretches. Wings slap
his body three times.
"COCK-AH-ha" pierces
dewed air — "COCK-AH-ha"
ricochets adobe walls
in empty brick and dirt streets.

Meters away heads, red combs,
slope to sky. Each alpha holds
his domain, opens his beak
cries same ancestral call
of verbal threats. AHs clash
COCKS, ha-s smack
AHs until sun burns land.

Flightless creatures
fold legs under their bodies
close eyes in territories
with unchanged boundaries,
same lords control.

Messages of Red (Part II)

Amidst green foliage
monkeys' eyes target
pomegranates. Fruit tempts
them to tear peels.
Teeth break
juice blisters
seeds crunch,
slurp sugars, vitamins to brains,
hit as if espresso.

Messages of Red (Part III)

Roses on Valentine's Day
combine with Merlot sips
and wet tongues travel lips
widen veins under skin.
Rushing blood flushes flesh
spreads warmth swells organs
between the thighs.

Addicts

We chase words
catch the luring
move them around
for readers' seduction.

Calls Himself Agnostic

(Dedicated for George Mathon)

He crosses his legs,
shakes the hanging foot,
rubs his hand like two sticks
to flick a spark, ignite a dried desert bush.
He says,
When I finish a poem, I feel like God.

Hours each day his back bends
into the couch, laptop on his lap,
fingers thump keys
he mumbles a chant
then words make imagery;
Wood Storks' beaks clamp
frighten fish. Chicks in nest cry for food.
Pelicans dive for guts, fishermen toss.

Lines later he
landmarks his beliefs
like churches
temples of a new world
in pueblos' square
Spaniards built
over indigenous altars.

God, this self-claimed agnostic says
I will believe
if proven, but
no one can. His next poem
preaches there should be
an eleventh commandment
"none of the above."

Between Texarkana and Dallas

In a roadside café,
the smoking half exhales smog
diffuses into nonsmoking half,
tears your eyes. Inside the haze
quarters roll into jukebox.
Country music twangs.

Wrinkles rut the outside corners
of waitress eyes
whose white apron shields
the lap of her white dress. She serves
two eggs over-easy, white toast, ham
and grits. Melted margarine puddles
its crater. Pepper specs float.

We pay cash at the beige Formica counter,
climb into the Corps of Engineers tan van,
drive Interstate 30.
Pass livestock auction barns
— western clothing stores
— billboards' lures to
cowboy churches in prefab buildings
where pastors bellow benedictions
and buckaroos carol *Happy Trails to You.*

Flying Shit I Swallowed

> "Limpia" is the technique of spiritual cleansing using an egg.
> It takes on energy. - Shaeen Miro Insight Blog

Joy wears sarong knotted on her belly,
stands in pavilion. The curandera
walks around her, drips rose water.
Her casted Circle traps Joy's energy,
good & bad. I and other students watch
the curandera holds an egg
an inch above Joy's head,
glides to her naked breasts. Halts.
Egg sucks crap from Joy's insides
until full. The overflow shit smacks
collapses the casted Circle's wall,
shoots over rubble
seeks me, finds me.
As if, I swallowed sour milk
my stomach muscles constrict, purge.

Tantric Dance in the Drum Circle

Drums tingle air fire warms,
hands swirl heavens' spirits,
toes swish sand
between their gaps, grainy particles
polish soles, solo bodies twirl
and brush others.

Her slanted eyes catch mine.

Breath apart in the space we secure
passerby dancers do not enter.
Palms to palms over our heads,
fingers interlace.
Electrons and protons stream the loop.
Positive and negative charges pull.
Nipples touch.

Vibrations trill our minds. Inhalations
fill stomachs. Mmms in steamy air exhale
on ears, necks and bellies.

Our arms fall and wrap the other's waists.
I hold her buttocks. She holds mine.
Hips swing,
                    thrust us
to the Milky Way's glow.

Stimulation

D says,
whiskey makes my nipples hard,
then lifts and tilts the metal flask.
Her lips glued to the spiral stub
tighter than its cap,
then passes the spirits to me
pulls her shirt over her head.
Fire's glow reddens
areolas. Auras halo
her nipples. They grow,
time-lapsed flowers at dawn.

Haiku

My fingers slide an ice chip
on her bare back, butter
on a griddle melts.

At the Pagan Spirit Gathering

Gale pushes grey, gust billows black
over us. Tirger lily in panties
and I naked sit on an air mattress
in her van, eat sunflower butter
spread on rice crackers
with an apple our teeth snap
while we wait

for thunder crack clouds.

Rain in wind hits the vehicle.
She rolls the door. Latch catches.

I rub her feet and legs below the knees.
Then we lie, head next to head
with a line of air between us,
study drops weep on windows.

Tiger springs, hisses, "I'm bored."
I say, "Read me a story."
She opens a book
flashlight circles words
      does not recite.

Reading Anaïs Nin's Little Birds

I click
the switch
of a floor lamp,
sit,
grab the hardcover
spread it.
Florescence shines
on pages
with a sandstone friction
sewn in red binder.
As chair cushions
butt and bottoms of thighs,
Anaïs straddles my lap. Her arms
on my shoulders. Her hands clutch
back of my neck. Lips lip.
Tongues lick. My wants bulge
spill its desire.

Contortion

This wooer wishes to bathe
with the contortionist
in a pond
under the full moon,
which is tonight.

If he could, they would
bend
twist
glide soap
to, then beyond
each other's curves.

If she would, he would
let hands and feet
rise, circle, trickle.
Toes squeeze sponge.
Squirt drops.

Outside of Reach

In zero gravity the son
of an astronaut
and contortionist
squeezes into a strand
ties knots
along and at his ends,
unlaces, bows and flips.

An eye muscle's twitch
propels the spacewalker
with its umbilical cord
to the lens' backside

reemerges under a membrane
the floater cannot penetrate.

Contact Stays Severed

Naked from night's sleep
        spurred by caffeine
I walk towards her.
  My arms circle waist.
      Lips kiss,
      eyes tell a hope.
She in t-shirt and pants
steps one bare foot
behind her back then the other.
She asserts her reminder,
You Don't Get It.

To myself I say
I won't till she tells me.
Silence hushes my ego
mutes my desire.

Prudence

> Dear Prudence,
> won't you come out to play?
> - Lennon/McCartney

You will not leave your house
on a snowy day and slip on ice,
nor walk on the grass because your big toe
might slip and break in a mole hole,
nor squish mud with your bare feet
give the gunk a chance to turn your ankle.

You might as well hang out
with Palermo's wealthy
in the catacombs
beneath the Capuchin Monastery
with a boned neck, hands, feet,
all of your smiling teeth in your skull
like the others display
inside a niche in the wall
draped in their best suits, clergy robes
as you drink cappuccino
with the elite women in dresses,
a section separated from men.

It doesn't matter if I see you naked
and if we get intimate, with your x-rays.
Because, I know your bones stayed whole.
Mine splintered, healed with scars.

Spilled Wishes

Left hand grabs the brown bottle
right twists plastic cap
glued to a cork. Plug squeaks
above twelve-year-old scotch
where the whiskey waits
to breathe
decanting
like a genie
trapped in stuffy air.
She asks what she can grant.
Knuckles knock the glass
before I answer.

The Crave to Purge and Keep

Urges tumble inside my brain.
I sort what did not break
and categorize things I think
I will want to retrieve
as how librarians shelve books.

Under the relics' fragments,
I find an earthen vessel
filled with red wine. I drink,

get drunk throw the empty jug.
It crashes on the marble floor, spatters.
The clay's edges and curves
crumble between my fingers

the way my body
smashes wrinkled sheets
absorbed with fluids
she and I secreted.
I will inhale the perfume tonight.

Insomniac's Relief

I tell myself
10:30PM go to bed, yawn
plead for the man
to throw sand in my eyes
then command,
fingers pull eyelids.
My mind spins the crank
inside the shaft
of the carnival's ride.
The *Wave Swinger* gouges
sunset. Orange heat burns
hemp rope knotted to pole's top
and the board where I sit. I fall
into unruly meeting. Everyone yells
over the others. Their repeats echo
what I should have done, need to do.
Sharp words cut my veins
till the pill dulls voices
lets my blood drain.

Salvatore Marici is the author of the chapbook *Mortals, Nature, and their Spirits* and a poetry collection entitled *Swish Swirl & Sniff.* He was the Midwest Writing Center's 2010 Poet-in-Resident. His poetry has appeared in *Toasted Cheese, Descant* (Canadian publication), *Spillway, Prairie Gold: An Anthology of the American Heartland, Earth's Daughter* and many others journals, magazines, and anthologies. In addition, both the Lee County Alliance for the Arts and the Midwest Writing Center have published broadsides of his poems. He has won several poetry contests, judged poetry contests, and taught poetry workshops. Marici served as a Peace Corps volunteer in Guatemala and is a civil servant retiree as an agronomist.

Acknowledgments

Amid Life—NPR Based http://www.npr.org/sections/parallels/2015/11/16/456213887/amid-mourning-life-in-paris-goes-on

From the Ether—"Her lips came together and smiled mysteriously." Last line in *The Grapes of Wrath* by John Steinbeck

Stuck after six hours of Socializing—"Of course, they want to be alone." Last line of *Red Pony* by John Steinbeck. "Of course," she said to herself." Second to last line of *Red Pony* by John Steinbeck.

He Calls Himself an Agnostic—"As a frightened fish swims away from its feet, it bumps into the bird's beak. The sensitive beak can feel the fish, and it clamps down on it within a fraction of a second." From https://www.nps.gov/ever/learn/nature/birds.htm

The Ice Cube Press began publishing in 1993 to focus on how to live with the natural world. We've since become devoted to using the literary arts to better understand how people can best live together in the communities they share, inhabit, and experience here in the Heartland of the USA. We have been recognized by a number of well-known writers including: Gary Snyder, Gene Logsdon, Wes Jackson, Patricia Hampl, Greg Brown, Jim Harrison, Annie Dillard, Ken Burns, Roz Chast, Jane Hamilton, Daniel Menaker, Kathleen Norris, Janisse Ray, Robert Hass, Alison Deming, Frank Deford, Paul Hawken, Harriet Lerner, Richard Rhodes, Michael Pollan, David Abram, David Orr, Boria Sax, and Barry Lopez. We've published a number of well-known authors including: Governor Robert Ray, Congressman James Leach, Mary Swander, Jim Heynen, Mary Pipher, Bill Holm, Connie Mutel, John T. Price, Carol Bly, Marvin Bell, Debra Marquart, Ted Kooser, Stephanie Mills, Bill McKibben, Craig Lesley, Elizabeth McCracken, Dean Bakopoulos, Dan Gable, Rick Bass, Pam Houston, and Paul Gruchow. Check out Ice Cube Press books on our web site, join our facebook group, follow us on twitter, visit booksellers, museum shops, or any place you can find good books and discover why we continue striving to, "hear the other side."

Ice Cube Press, LLC (Est. 1993)
North Liberty, Iowa 52317-9302
steve@icecubepress.com
twitter: @icecubepress
www.facebook.com/IceCubePress
www.IceCubePress.com

to Fenna Marie
your very being is
a beautiful and glorious
positive proof of creation
I love you!